The Step-by-Step Way to Draw Unicorn

A Fun and Easy Drawing Book to Learn How to Draw Unicorns

By

Kristen Diaz.

License Notes

Table of Contents

Introduction

Becoming a great artist requires creativity, patience and practice. These habits can flourish in children when they start to develop them at a young age. We believe our guide will teach your child the discipline and patience required to not just learn to draw well, but to use those qualities in everything they do. Your job as a parent is to work with your child and encourage them when stuck and feel like giving up.

The world of art is an amazing way for you and your child to communicate and bond. When you open this book and start to create with your little one, you will delight in the things you learn about them and they will feel closer to you. Your support and gentle suggestions will help them be more patient with themselves and soon they will take the time needed to create spectacular drawings of which you can both be proud.

This guide is useful for parents as it teaches fundamentals of drawing and simple techniques. By following this book with your child, adults will learn patience and develop their skills as a child's most important teacher. By spending a few hours together you will develop a strong connection and learn the best ways of communicating with each other. It is truly a rewarding experience when you and your child create a masterpiece by working together!

How to draw a unicorn 1

Step 1.

Draw a small circle for the head and two big ones for the chest and the hips. Add a rectangle for the snout and two triangles for the ears. Then add the outline for the tail.

Step 2.

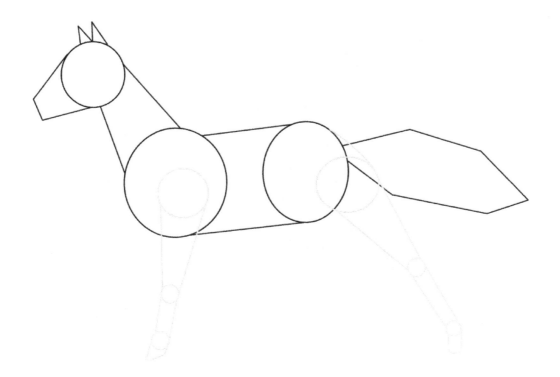

Add a circle for the shoulder, knee and ankle joints. Connect
them to the body and add the outline for the hooves.

Step 3.

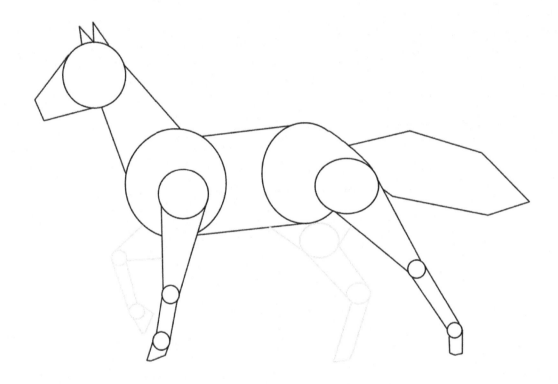

The other front leg is moving upwards, while the hind leg stands firmly on the ground. Use the example to help you draw the remaining legs.

Step 4.

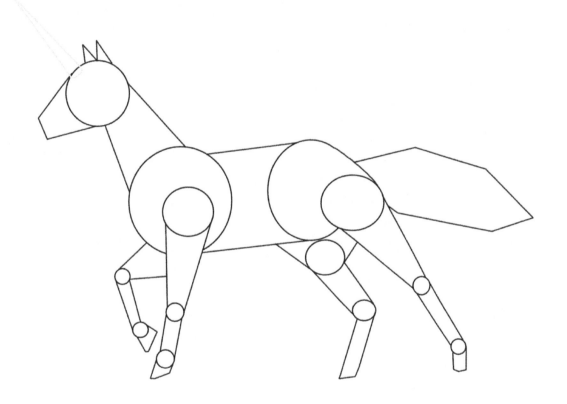

Add a sharp spike to the front of the head.

Step 5.

Redraw the head. Smooth out the nose, mouth and jaw and add a big nostril. Add a small eye and curve out the ears.

Step 6.

Now we will reshape the body. Start by drawing the neck down to the chest. Draw the back into a wavy shape and curve out the stomach. Use the example the help you along.

Step 7.

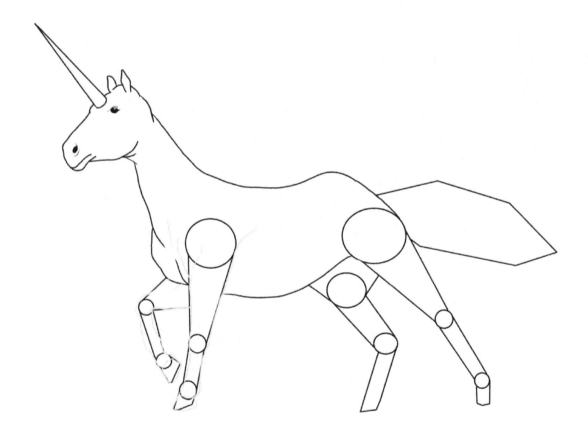

Let's go to the legs. Reshape the two front legs as in the example.

Make sure to add a small portion of the skin over the hooves.

Step 8.

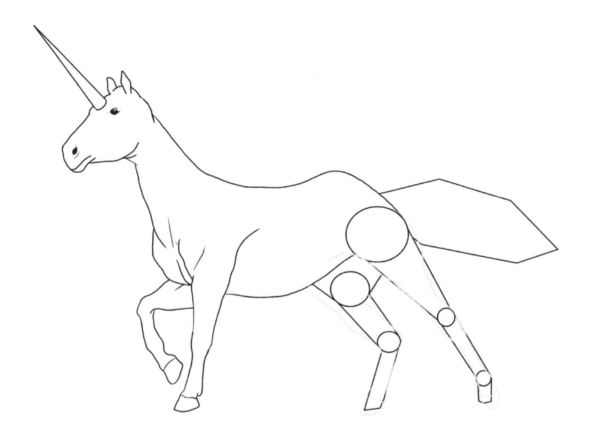

Now for the rear legs. Redraw them so they curve nicely unto the body as in the example. Don't forget to check the hooves.

Step 9.

Now for the horn. This unicorn has a horn that spirals upwards into a sharp point. Use the example to help you along.

Step 10.

Now add a wave mane to the neck and a wave hair to the tail.

Add some spots to the body to give it different colors.

The unicorn is a strong animal, so add some lines to show where the muscles are hiding.

Step 12.

All done! Let's color!

Step 13.

This unicorn is usually of light colors. The fur is light brown, but the hair is dark still. The spots are a slightly lighter caller of brown. The horn is orange. Color yours however you feel like!

Step 14.

Add some shadow for more volume.

Step 15.

Colored version.

Step 16.

Line art.

How to draw a unicorn 2

Step 1.

Draw a small circle for the head and two big ones for the chest and the hips. Add a rectangle for the snout and two triangles for the ears. Then add the outline for the tail.

Step 2.

Add a circle for the shoulder, knee and ankle joints. Connect them to the body and add the outline for the hooves.

Step 3.

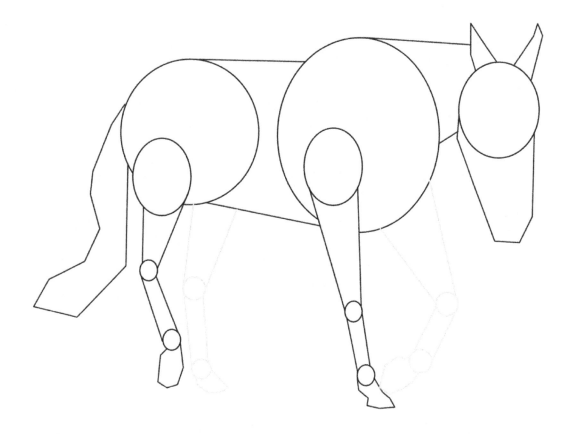

The other front leg is moving upwards, while the hind leg stands firmly on the ground. Use the example to help you draw the remaining legs.

Step 4.

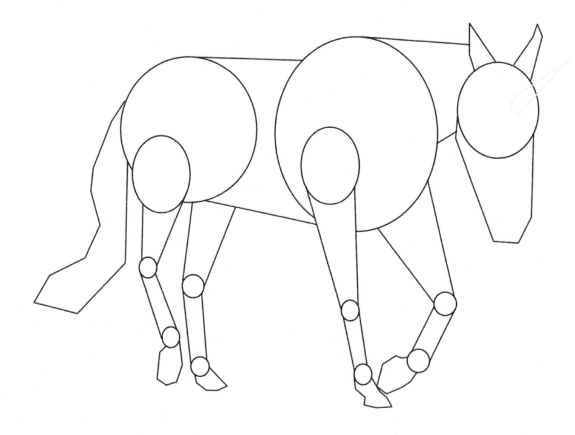

Add a sharp spike to the front of the head.

Step 5.

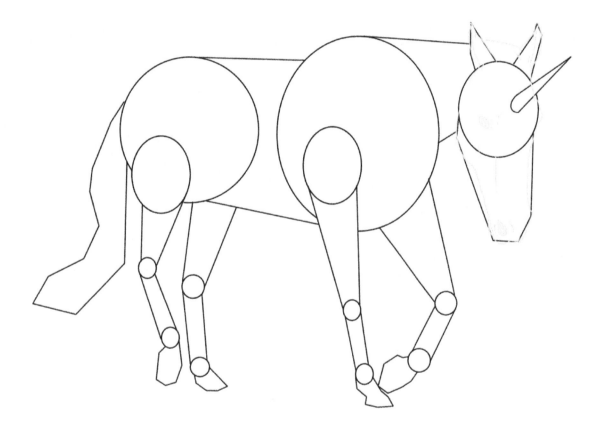

Redraw the head. Smooth out the nose, mouth and jaw and add a big nostril. Add a small eye and curve out the ears.

Step 6.

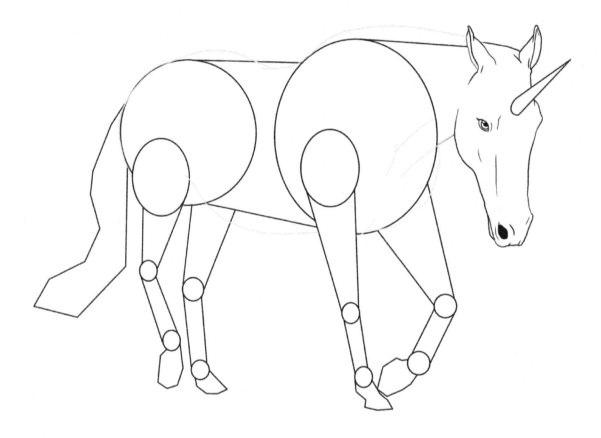

Now we will reshape the body. Start by drawing the neck down to the chest. Draw the back into a wavy shape and curve out the stomach. Use the example the help you along.

Step 7.

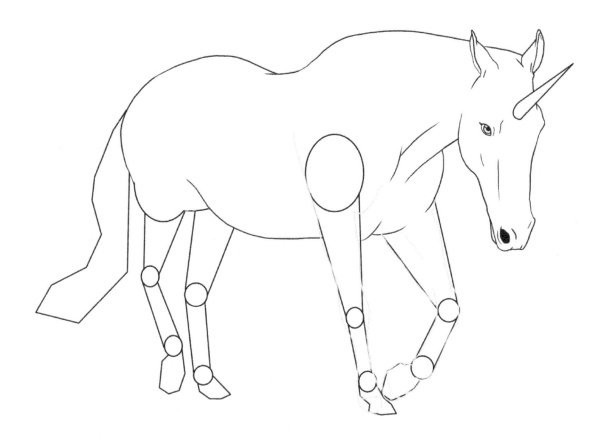

Let's go to the legs. Reshape the two front legs as in the example.

Make sure to add a small portion of the skin over the hooves.

Step 8.

Now for the rear legs. Redraw them so they curve nicely unto the body as in the example. Don't forget to check the hooves.

Step 9.

Now for the horn. This unicorn has a horn that wobbles from thick to thin into a sharp point at the end. Use the example to help you along.

Step 10.

Now add soft spikes to the mane to the neck and a wavy hair to the tail. Add some spots to the body to give it different colors.

Step 11.

The unicorn is a strong animal, so add some lines to show where the muscles are hiding.

Step 12.

All done! Let's color!

Step 13.

This unicorn is usually of light colors. The fur is light pink, but the hair is dark red. The spots are a slightly lighter caller of brown. The horn is made of gold and the eyes blue. Color yours however you feel like!

Step 14.

Add some shadow for more volume.

Step 15.

Colored version.

Step 16.

Line art.

How to draw a unicorn 3

Step 1.

Draw a small circle for the head and two big ones for the chest and the hips. Add a rectangle for the snout and two triangles for the ears. Then add the outline for the tail.

Step 2.

Add a circle for the shoulder, knee and ankle joints. Connect them to the body and add the outline for the hooves.

Step 3.

Both rear legs swing forward, giving the impression that it is running. Use the example to help you draw the remaining legs.

Step 4.

Add a sharp spike to the front of the head.

Step 5.

Redraw the head and add the neck line connecting to the body. Smooth out the nose, mouth and jaw and add a big nostril. Add a small eye and curve out the ears.

Step 6.

Now we will reshape the body. Start by drawing the neck a little wider, down to the chest. Draw the back into a wavy shape and curve out the stomach. Use the example the help you along.

Step 7.

Let's go to the legs. Reshape the two front legs as in the example.

Make sure to add a small portion of the skin over the hooves.

Step 8.

Now for the rear legs. Redraw them so they curve nicely unto the
body as in the example. Don't forget to check the hooves.

Step 9.

Now for the horn. This unicorn has a horn that wobbles from thick to thin into a sharp point at the end. Use the example to help you along.

Step 10.

Now add soft spikes to the mane to the neck and a wavy hair to the tail.

Step 11.

The unicorn is a strong animal, so add some lines to show where the muscles are hiding.

Step 12.

All done! Let's color!

Step 13.

This unicorn is usually of light colors. The fur is light orange, and the hair light brown. The horn is red. Color yours however you feel like!

Step 14.

Add some shadow for more volume.

Step 15.

Colored version.

Step 16.

Line art.

About the Author

Kristen Diaz is an accomplished artist and e-book author living in Southern California. She has provided the illustrations for hundreds of children's books as her realistic and lifelike images appeal to children and adults alike.

Diaz began her career as an artist when she was in her 20's creating caricatures on the beaches of sunny California. What started as a way to make extra spending money turned into a successful career because of her amazing talent. Her comically accurate caricatures had a unique look and one of the local authors took notice. When the writer asked Diaz to illustrate one of her books, Kristen jumped at the opportunity to showcase her talent. The result was spectacular and soon Diaz was in high demand. Her ability to change her style to fit the books made her an attractive artist to work with.

She decided to get a more formal education in graphic design and illustration by enrolling in the Arts program at Platt's College which is where she met the love of her life and life partner, Terri. The two live in Pasadena close to the beach where Diaz' career first flourished. She occasionally hangs out on the beach with her easel and paints and makes caricatures of the humanity passing by. Her e-books are simple to follow and contain many witty anecdotes about her life in Pasadena.

Made in the USA
Coppell, TX
17 April 2020

20608991R00033